U.S.A. TRAVEL GUIDES

FLORIDA

BY ANN HEINRICHS • ILLUSTRATED BY MATT KANIA

The Child's World®
childsworld.com

Published by The Child's World®
1980 Lookout Drive • Mankato, MN 56003-1705
800-599-READ • www.childsworld.com

Photo Credits

Photographs ©: iStockphoto, cover, 1, 19, 24; Shutterstock
Images, 7, 8, 27; Rudy Umans/Shutterstock Images, 11;
Nick Fox/Shutterstock Images, 12; Mingo Hagen CC2.0,
15; Walter CC2.0, 16; Edwin Verin/Shutterstock Images,
20; Florida Keys Public Library CC2.0, 21; Travis Wise
CC2.0, 23; Action Sports Photography/Shutterstock
Images, 28; P. Clark/iStockphoto, 31; J. A. Tillard/
Shutterstock Images, 32; G. Johnston Photo/iStockphoto,
35; Atlas Pix/Shutterstock Images, 37 (left), 37 (right)

ISBN 9781503819498
LCCN 2016961126

Printing

Printed in the United States of America
PA02334

Ann Heinrichs is the author
of more than 100 books
for children and young
adults. She has also enjoyed
successful careers as a
children's book editor and
an advertising copywriter.
Ann grew up in Fort Smith,
Arkansas, and lives in
Chicago, Illinois.

post card

About the Author
Ann Heinrichs

Matt Kania loves maps and, as a
kid, dreamed of making them. In
school he studied geography and
cartography, and today he makes
maps for a living. Matt's favorite
thing about drawing maps is
learning about the places they
represent. Many of the maps
he has created can be found in
books, magazines, videos, Web
sites, and public places.

post card

About the
Map Illustrator
Matt Kania

On the cover: Visit one of Florida's beautiful beaches.

OUR FLORIDA TRIP

FLORIDA

Ready for a tour of the Sunshine State? You'll find plenty to see and do there. You'll meet alligators and manatees. You'll dance in the streets and spit watermelon seeds. You'll explore space and the underwater world. Just follow the dotted line or skip around. Either way, you're in for an exciting ride. Are you all buckled up? Then we're on our way!

WELCOME TO **FLORIDA**

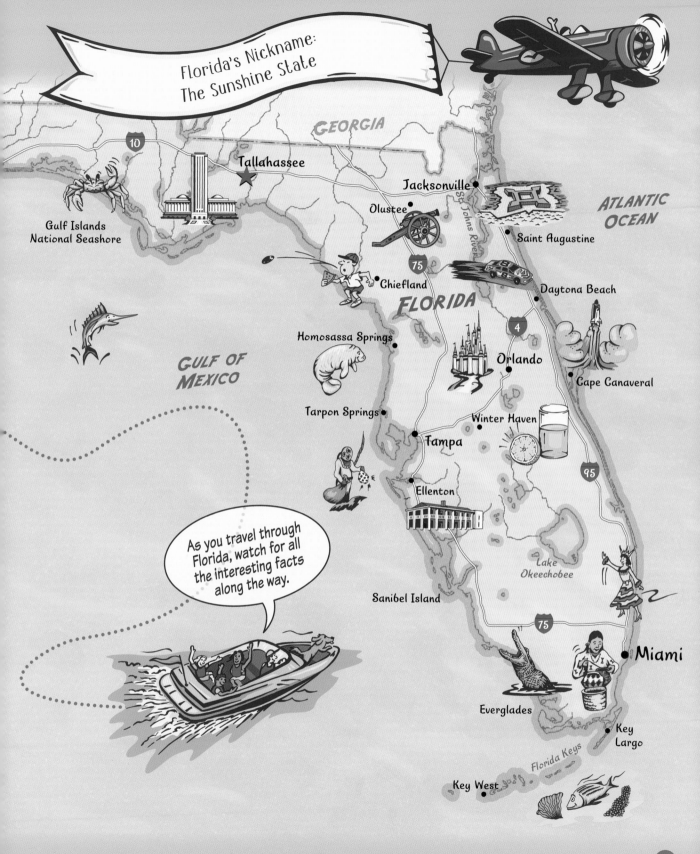

Florida's Nickname:
The Sunshine State

GEORGIA

10   Tallahassee

Jacksonville

Olustee

Gulf Islands
National Seashore

Saint Augustine

ATLANTIC
OCEAN

75

Chiefland

FLORIDA

Daytona Beach

Homosassa Springs

4

Orlando

GULF OF
MEXICO

Cape Canaveral

Tarpon Springs

Winter Haven

Tampa

95

Ellenton

As you travel through
Florida, watch for all
the interesting facts
along the way.

Lake
Okeechobee

Sanibel Island

75

Miami

Everglades

Key
Largo

Florida Keys

Key West

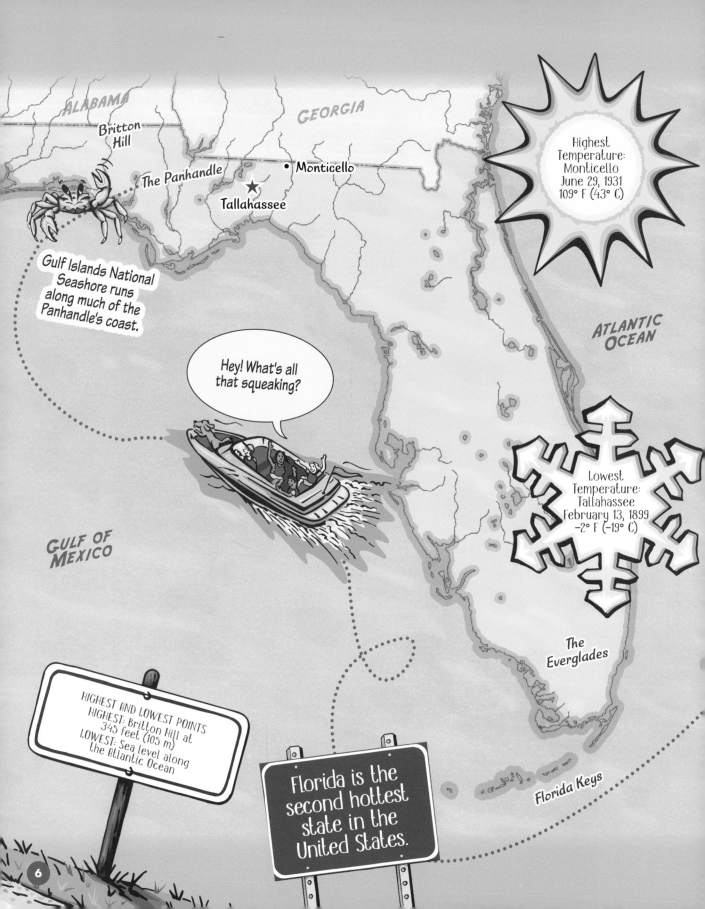

ALABAMA

GEORGIA

Britton Hill

The Panhandle

• Monticello

★ Tallahassee

Gulf Islands National Seashore runs along much of the Panhandle's coast.

Highest Temperature: Monticello June 29, 1931 109° F (43° C)

ATLANTIC OCEAN

Hey! What's all that squeaking?

Lowest Temperature: Tallahassee February 13, 1899 –2° F (–19° C)

GULF OF MEXICO

The Everglades

HIGHEST AND LOWEST POINTS
HIGHEST: Britton Hill at 345 feet (105 m)
LOWEST: Sea level along the Atlantic Ocean

Florida is the second hottest state in the United States.

Florida Keys

SQUEAKY SAND AND THE PANHANDLE

Take a step. Squeak! You're in the Florida Panhandle. And you're strolling along the beach. The sand squeaks when you walk on it! That is because the grains of sand are in a perfect oval shape, which cause them to squeak when walked on.

Northwestern Florida is long and thin. It's called the Panhandle. Just imagine grabbing it like you'd grab a frying pan!

Most of Florida is a **peninsula**. The Atlantic Ocean is on the east. On the west is the Gulf of Mexico. The Everglades is a big **marshland**. It covers most of southern Florida. Islands called the Florida Keys lie off the southern coast.

Don't forget your sunscreen! Florida is famous for its beaches.

CRITTERS IN THE EVERGLADES

Snap! There goes a fish. Chomp! There goes a frog. Watch out. That alligator looks hungry.

You're on a boat ride through the Everglades. You see turtles, snakes, and long-legged birds. Now you're face-to-face with an alligator. Keep your hands inside that boat!

The Everglades are full of animals. There are bobcats, manatees, and storks. Mangrove trees grow there, too. Spanish moss hangs down from their branches. Palm trees sway along the coast. Out in the water are fish and dolphins.

More than 200,000 alligators live in the Everglades. Florida is home to 1.5 million altogether!

ALABAMA

GEORGIA

Guess what? Alligators can't chew. They swallow their food whole. Kids, don't try this at home!

STATE FLOWER
ORANGE BLOSSOM

STATE TREE
SABAL PALM

STATE BIRD
MOCKINGBIRD

GULF OF MEXICO

ATLANTIC OCEAN

Tampa

Pelican Island

Busch Gardens is in Tampa. It has more than 12,000 animals living in their natural **habitats**.

The National Park Service has 11 sites in Florida.

The Everglades

The tiny Key deer lives only in the Florida Keys. It measures 24 to 32 inches (61 to 81 cm) at the shoulder.

Pelican Island was the country's first wildlife refuge. It was set aside in 1903. Brown pelicans, herons, and egrets live there.

Florida Keys

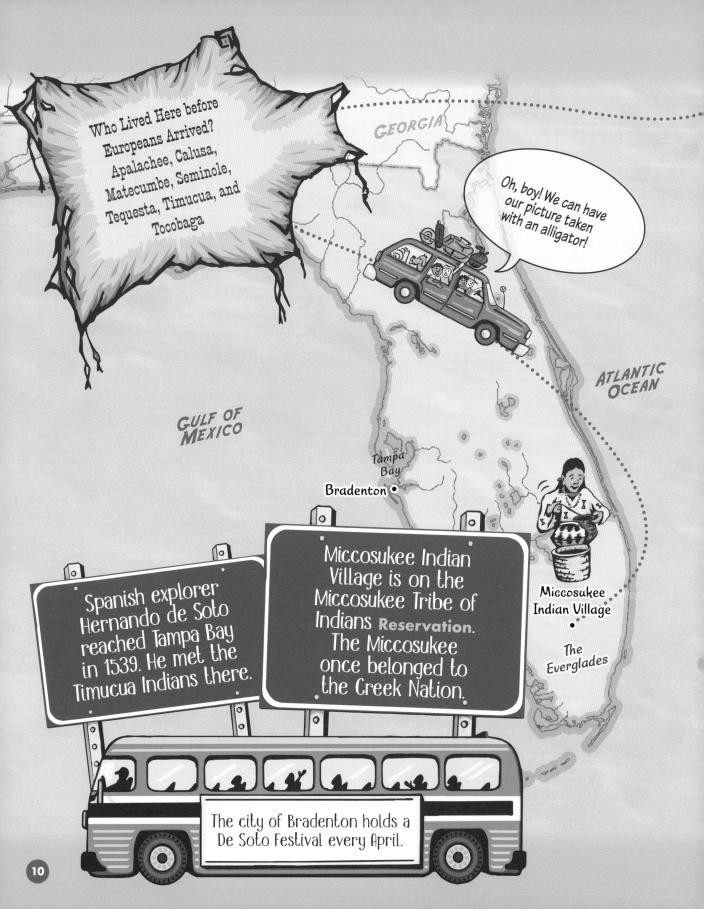

Who Lived Here before Europeans Arrived? Apalachee, Calusa, Matecumbe, Seminole, Tequesta, Timucua, and Tocobaga

GEORGIA

Oh, boy! We can have our picture taken with an alligator!

ATLANTIC OCEAN

GULF OF MEXICO

Tampa Bay

Bradenton

Miccosukee Indian Village

The Everglades

Spanish explorer Hernando de Soto reached Tampa Bay in 1539. He met the Timucua Indians there.

Miccosukee Indian Village is on the Miccosukee Tribe of Indians Reservation. The Miccosukee once belonged to the Creek Nation.

The city of Bradenton holds a De Soto Festival every April.

MICCOSUKEE INDIAN VILLAGE IN THE EVERGLADES

A villager enters the alligator pit. He grabs the gator, and *fwap*! The gator is on its back and can't move!

You're visiting Miccosukee Indian Village. The alligator show is fun to watch. But don't miss the rest of the village. It shows how Florida's Miccosukee Tribe of Indians once lived. You'll see villagers weaving baskets and carving wood. And you'll visit their chickees, or huts.

Many Native American groups are from Florida. Their lives changed forever in the 1500s. That's when Spanish explorers arrived. The Spaniards killed many Native Americans in battle. They also passed on diseases to them. Then in the 1830s, thousands were kicked out of their homes to make room for European settlers and forced to move west.

Miccosukee Indian Village gives visitors an insight into the Miccosukees' history and life today.

THE OLDEST WOODEN SCHOOLHOUSE AND SAINT AUGUSTINE

Yikes! You'd better be good in school today. You might be sent to the basement! Well, not really. You're visiting the Oldest Wooden Schoolhouse in the United States. It's located in Saint Augustine. Your guides are a mechanical teacher and students. They tell what their school day was like in the 1700s, and where naughty kids were sent!

Spaniards set up Saint Augustine in 1565. It's the oldest city in the United States. Spend a day in the city's old section. You'll see the jail and a fort. You can also visit people's homes. They show you what everyday life was like. And don't worry about that schoolhouse. It's a friendly place. You even get a **diploma** when you leave!

What was school like in the 1700s? Visit Saint Augustine and find out!

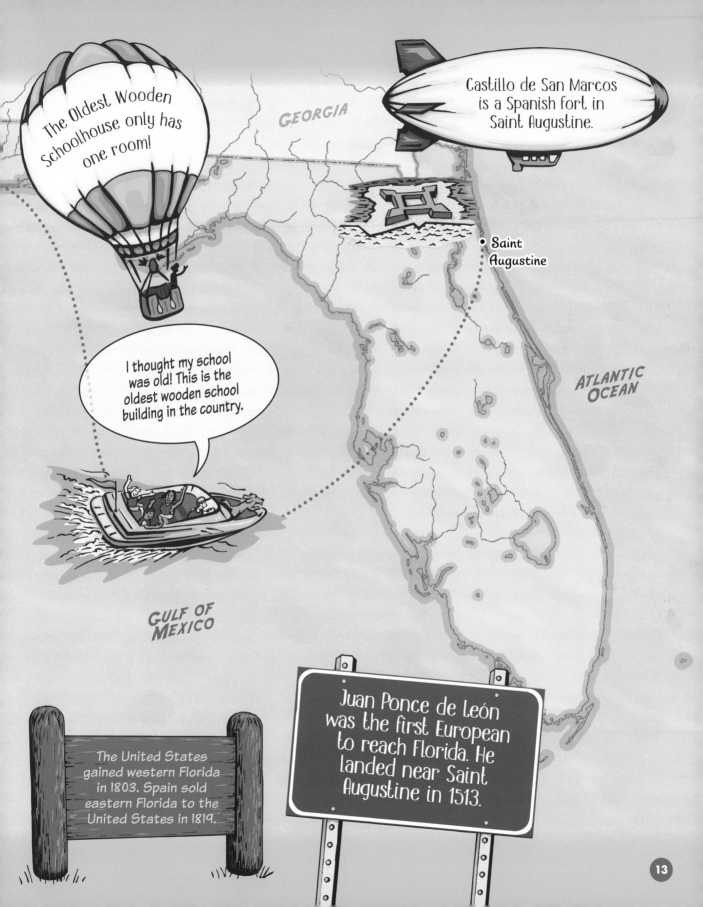

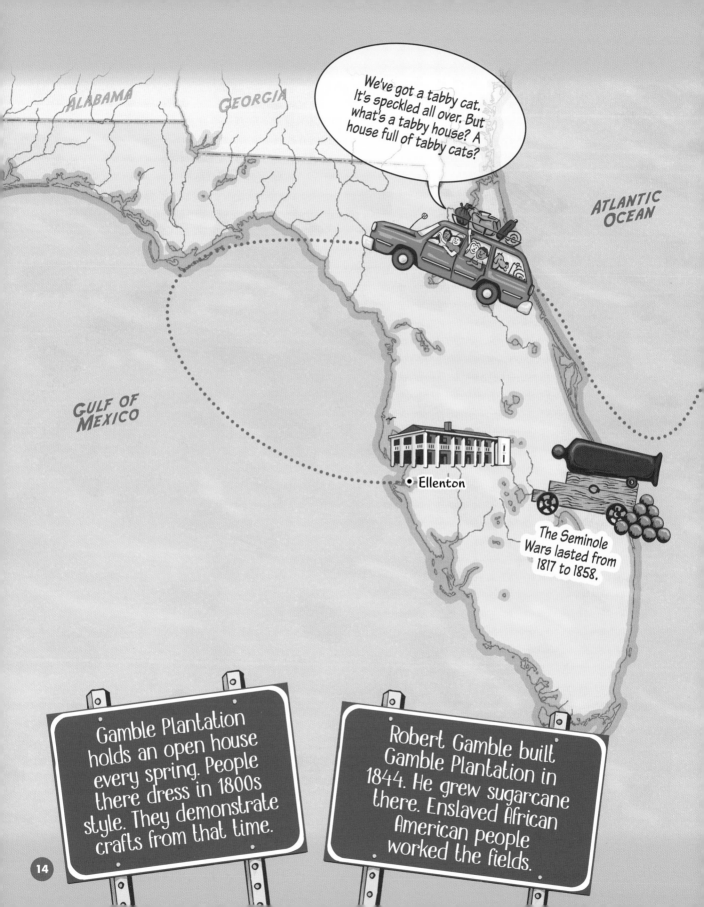

We've got a tabby cat. It's speckled all over. But what's a tabby house? A house full of tabby cats?

The Seminole Wars lasted from 1817 to 1858.

• Ellenton

Gamble Plantation holds an open house every spring. People there dress in 1800s style. They demonstrate crafts from that time.

Robert Gamble built Gamble Plantation in 1844. He grew sugarcane there. Enslaved African American people worked the fields.

The **mansion** at Ellenton's Gamble Plantation is a tabby house. That means its walls are made of tabby. Tabby is seashells mixed with sand.

Spain gave up Florida in 1819. Then American settlers poured in. Some built huge farms called plantations. They grew sugarcane and other crops. Many built their homes out of tabby.

European settlers wanted Native Americans out of the way. They wanted the Native American's land for farming. They forced the Seminole people off of their own land. The Seminole people fought hard to stay. This lead to three wars with the United States, later called the Seminole Wars. The Seminoles' leader, Chief Osceola, had them hide in the **swamps**. But most Seminoles were eventually driven out. Chief Osceola was thrown in jail for standing up for the Seminole people. He died a year later in jail.

The Gamble Plantation is the last standing plantation in southern Florida.

THE BATTLE OF OLUSTEE AND THE CIVIL WAR

Watch out! Cannons are booming! Men on horseback are swishing swords! It's the Battle of Olustee!

People act out this battle every year. It took place during the Civil War (1861–1865). Northern and Southern states fought this war over slavery. Florida joined the South, or Confederate side.

The Battle of Olustee was Florida's biggest Civil War battle. Confederates won the battle. But the North won the war. Then slaves were freed. But it was a long time before they gained rights.

Cannons, gunfire, and soldiers on horseback! People reenact the Battle of Olustee every February.

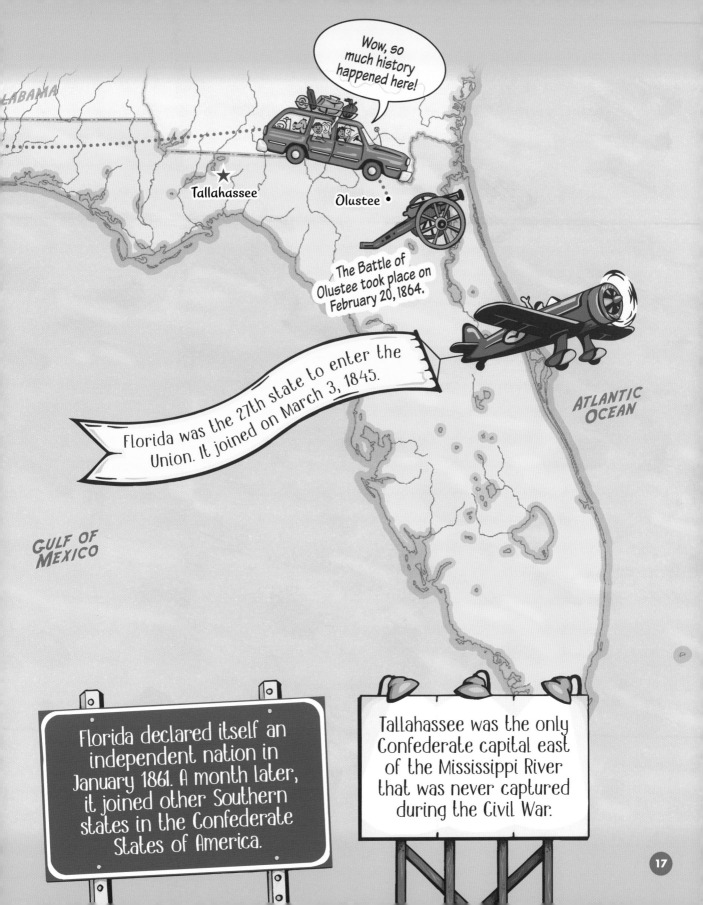

Wow, so much history happened here!

ALABAMA

★ Tallahassee

Olustee •

The Battle of Olustee took place on February 20, 1864.

Florida was the 27th state to enter the Union. It joined on March 3, 1845.

ATLANTIC OCEAN

GULF OF MEXICO

Florida declared itself an independent nation in January 1861. A month later, it joined other Southern states in the Confederate States of America.

Tallahassee was the only Confederate capital east of the Mississippi River that was never captured during the Civil War.

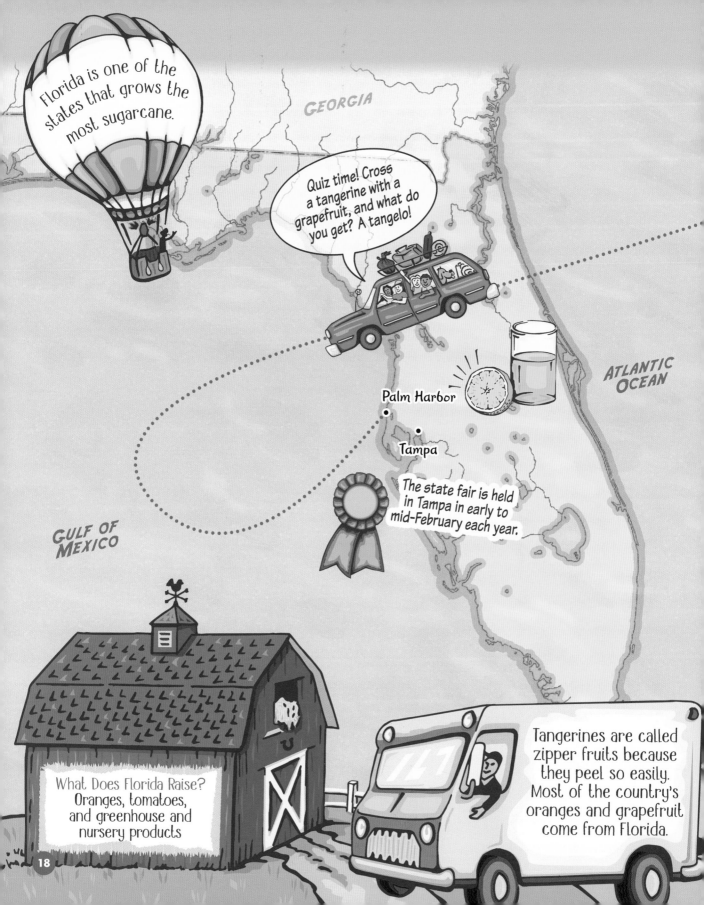

THE FLORIDA CITRUS FESTIVAL IN PALM HARBOR

Whoosh! There goes the roller coaster. Smash! That's the bumper cars. Glub, glub. That's no ride. It's the Jell-O eating contest!

You're at the Florida Citrus Festival in Palm Harbor. It celebrates Florida's top crops— citrus fruits. Railroads began bringing tourists to Florida in the 1880s. Swamps were drained to create more dry land. Then many farmers started growing citrus trees. They include oranges, grapefruits, and lemons. You know, the fruits that make your face squinch up!

Florida produces 70 percent of the oranges in the United States. That's a lot of oranges!

THE KENNEDY SPACE CENTER AT CAPE CANAVERAL

Fires blaze amid clouds of smoke. "Five, four, three, two, one. You are go for launch." The rocket blasts off into the sky! You're at the John F. Kennedy Space Center at Cape Canaveral. And you've just watched a rocket launch.

Kennedy Space Center opened in 1962. It became an important space center. Kennedy Space Center used to launch astronauts into space. However, it stopped in 2011. Now it just launches rockets. Visitors can tour the center.

Florida grew fast in the 1900s. Millions of people came as tourists. And millions moved there to live. Some came to take jobs in the state. Others came to retire in the warm climate.

Want to see a rocket launch? Visit the John F. Kennedy Space Center.

Cape Canaveral's space center sent the first U.S. astronauts to the Moon in 1969.

ALABAMA

GEORGIA

ATLANTIC OCEAN

Dear Mr. Flagler:

You built a railroad down the East Coast to Florida. You built hotels, too. That started Florida's tourism. You should see it now!

Gratefully,
A Beach Bum

post card

Mr. Henry Flagler
1830-1913
Whitehall
Palm Beach, FL

The coast near Cape Canaveral is called Florida's Space Coast.

• Merritt Island
• Cape Canaveral

GULF OF MEXICO

Palm Beach •

The space center is named after our 35th president. Talk about important!

Cape Canaveral is near Merritt Island. Merritt Island National Wildlife Refuge protects storks, sea turtles, and other wildlife.

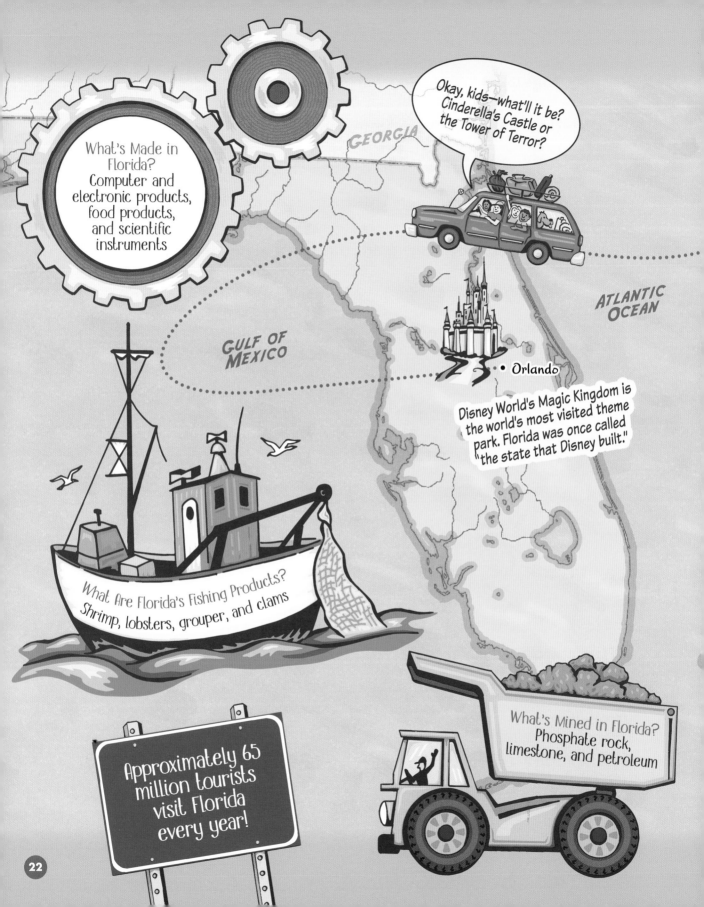

What's Made in Florida?
Computer and electronic products, food products, and scientific instruments

Okay, kids—what'll it be? Cinderella's Castle or the Tower of Terror?

GEORGIA

ATLANTIC OCEAN

GULF OF MEXICO

• Orlando

Disney World's Magic Kingdom is the world's most visited theme park. Florida was once called "the state that Disney built."

What Are Florida's Fishing Products?
Shrimp, lobsters, grouper, and clams

What's Mined in Florida?
Phosphate rock, limestone, and petroleum

Approximately 65 million tourists visit Florida every year!

WALT DISNEY WORLD IN ORLANDO

Eek! We're in The Twilight Zone Tower of Terror. We're plunging 13 stories down! And this is the Happiest Place on Earth? That's what some people say! It's Walt Disney World in Orlando. The Tower is located at the park's Hollywood Studios site.

Tourism is a big business in Florida. Millions of people visit Disney World every year. But Florida has lots of other **industries**, too. Its factories make computers, airplanes, and orange juice.

Florida's mines produce phosphate rock. The rock is made into **fertilizer**. Florida is a big fishing state, too. Just look at that long coastline!

Four theme parks make up Walt Disney World. Cinderella's castle at Magic Kingdom lights up every night!

THE SKYSCRAPER CAPITOL IN TALLAHASSEE

In most states, you can spot the state capitol. It's a few stories high. And it has a big, round **dome** on top. But Florida's capitol is a **skyscraper**. It's 22 stories high! And its roof is flat. You can take a tour to the top. Look around and you'll see for miles!

Many state government offices are in the capitol. Florida has three branches of government. One branch makes laws. Its members come from all over the state. The governor heads another branch. It carries out the laws. Courts make up the third branch. They decide whether someone has broken the law.

Florida's state capitol is unusual. It's one of America's four skyscraper capitols.

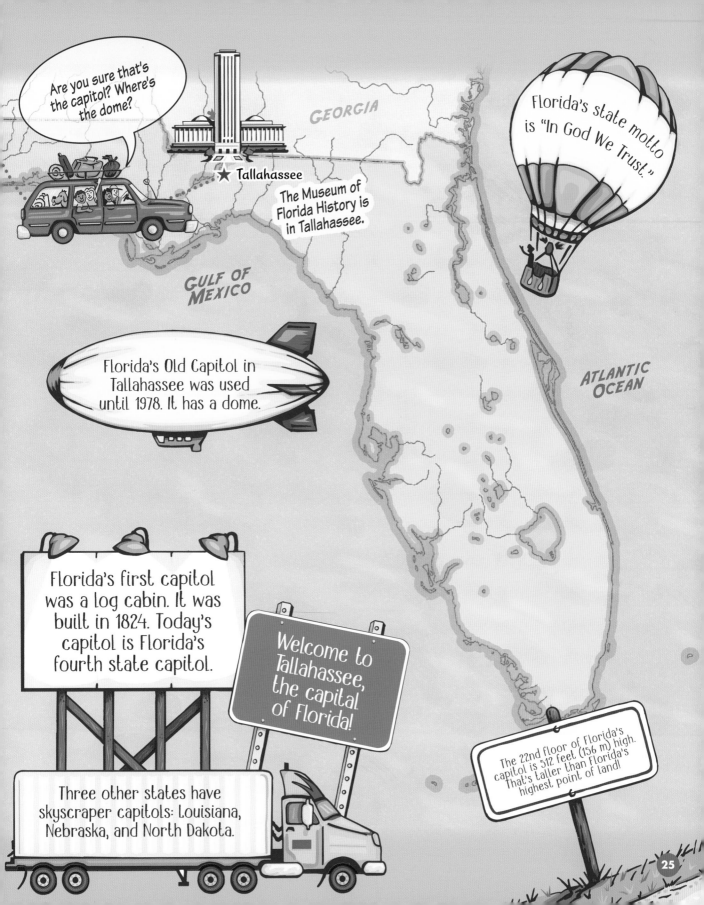

ALABAMA

GEORGIA

Little Havana is named after Havana, the capital of Cuba.

Jacksonville

ATLANTIC OCEAN

In 2016, 20,612,439 people lived in Florida. It's the third largest state by population.

Quiz time: What does Calle Ocho mean? It's Spanish for "Eighth Street"!

Tampa

Calle Ocho is the main street in Little Havana.

GULF OF MEXICO

Miami

POPULATION OF LARGEST CITIES

Jacksonville............... 868,031
Miami....................... 399,508
Tampa....................... 369,715

As of 2015, approximately 24 percent of Floridians are Hispanic or Latino. Approximately 17 percent of Floridians are African American.

Scarf down some **arepas**. Dance the **merengue**. Sneak between a stilt walker's legs. You're at Calle Ocho!

Calle Ocho began as a Cuban festival. Now it's the biggest **Hispanic** festival in the country. It's held in Miami's Little Havana neighborhood.

Florida is home to many Cubans, Haitians, and Jamaicans. Their homelands are islands south of Florida. Many older people retire to Florida, too. Florida's population just keeps on growing. Only two states have more people.

The Calle Ocho Festival is held in March every year.

DAYTONA USA

Vroom! You're up to 200 miles (322 km) an hour. Screech! You're rounding a corner four stories high. You're in the driver's seat at Daytona USA!

Daytona USA is a theme park for racing fans. It's right by the Daytona International Speedway in Daytona Beach. That's where the Daytona 500 car races are held. It's the official theme park of NASCAR!

Racing is just one of Florida's popular sports. Football fans enjoy the New Year's bowl games. Other people like quieter fun. They relax on the sunny beaches. They swim in the ocean. They watch wildlife or collect seashells. What would you do in Florida?

The race at the Daytona International Speedway takes 200 laps around the track to complete!

Gatorade is named after the Gators. They're the University of Florida's football team.

Hey . . . are you a speed demon? Then Daytona's the place for you!

GEORGIA

• Jacksonville

The world's only hamburger museum is in Daytona Beach.

Daytona Beach •

GULF OF MEXICO

• Orlando

ATLANTIC OCEAN

Tampa Bay

• Sarasota

Florida Football and Hockey Teams
Florida Panthers (hockey)
Jacksonville Jaguars (football)
Miami Dolphins (football)
Tampa Bay Buccaneers (football)
Tampa Bay Lightning (hockey)

Florida Baseball and Basketball Teams
Florida Marlins (baseball)
Miami Heat (basketball)
Orlando Magic (basketball)
Tampa Bay Rays (baseball)

• Miami

Florida's College Football Bowl Games
Buffalo Wild Wing Citrus Bowl—Orlando
TaxSlayer Bowl—Jacksonville
Capital One Orange Bowl—Miami

Circus founder John Ringling established the John and Mable Ringling Museum of Art in Sarasota. It has a fine collection of classic art.

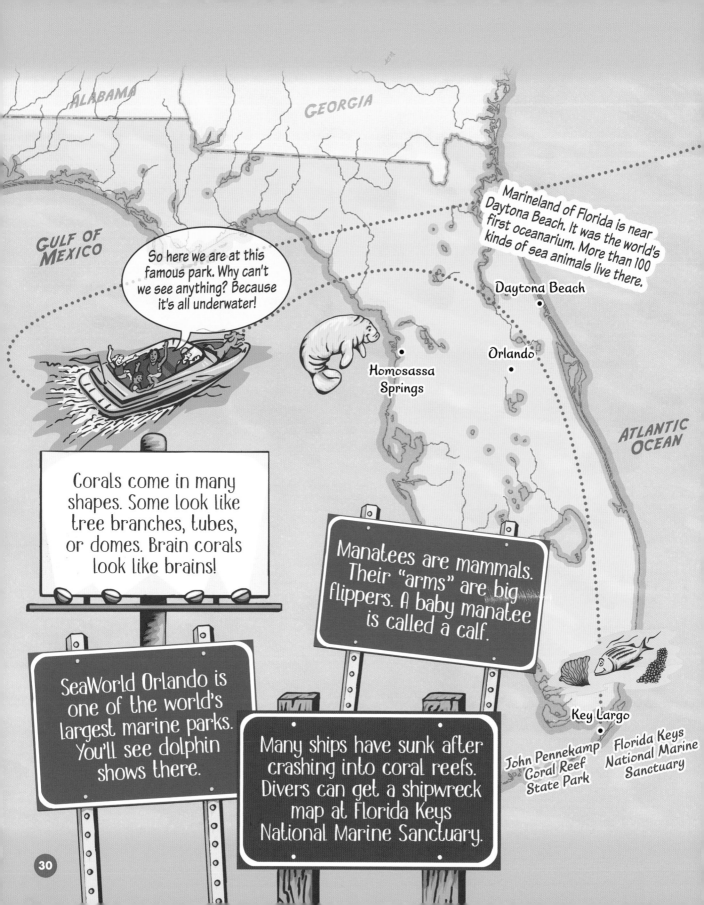

JOHN PENNEKAMP CORAL REEF STATE PARK

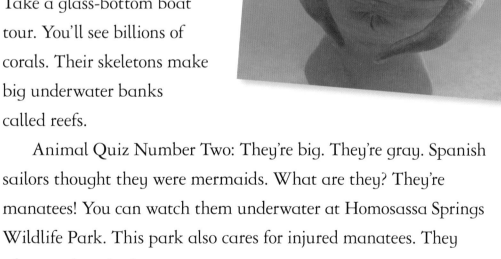

Animal Quiz Number One: It lives in the sea. It might be pink, orange, purple, or green. And its skeleton can sink ships. What is it? Coral! Just visit John Pennekamp Coral Reef State Park. It's in Key Largo. Take a glass-bottom boat tour. You'll see billions of corals. Their skeletons make big underwater banks called reefs.

Animal Quiz Number Two: They're big. They're gray. Spanish sailors thought they were mermaids. What are they? They're manatees! You can watch them underwater at Homosassa Springs Wildlife Park. This park also cares for injured manatees. They often get hurt by boats.

Manatees are nicknamed "sea cows." But they don't say moo!

SPONGES IN TARPON SPRINGS

Animal Quiz Number Three: It lives in the sea. It's full of holes. And it has no brain. What is it? It's a sea sponge!

Most sponges you see today are factory-made. But natural sponges are living things. Divers harvest the sponges from the sea.

Tarpon Springs is the sponge capital of the world. Greek **immigrants** settled there in the early 1900s. They were experts at diving for sponges. A local museum tells all about sponge diving. The museum is called Spongeorama!

Visit Tarpon Springs to see sea sponges pulled from the ocean!

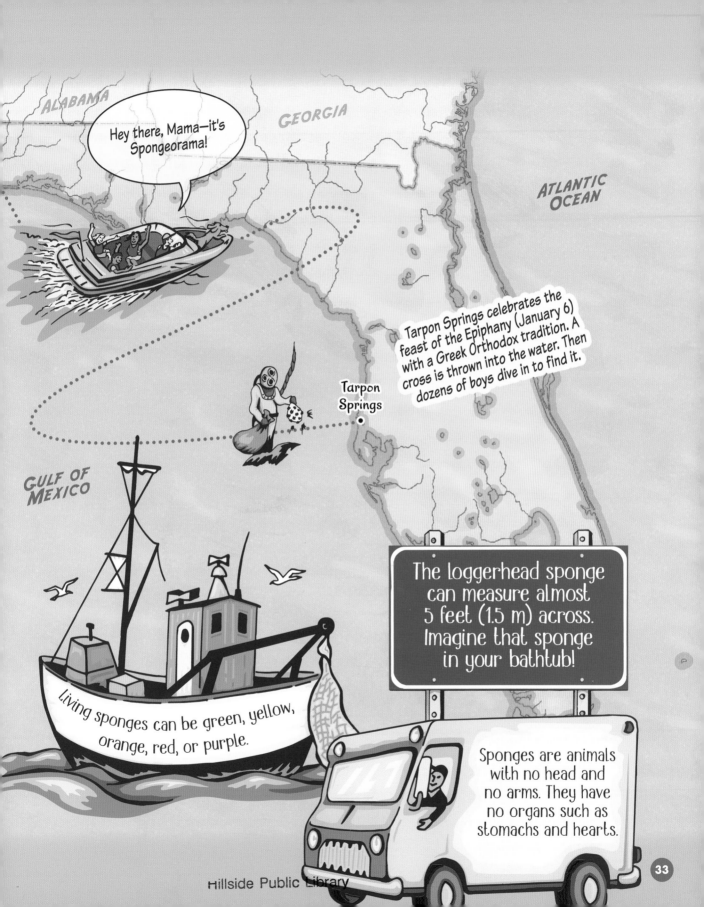

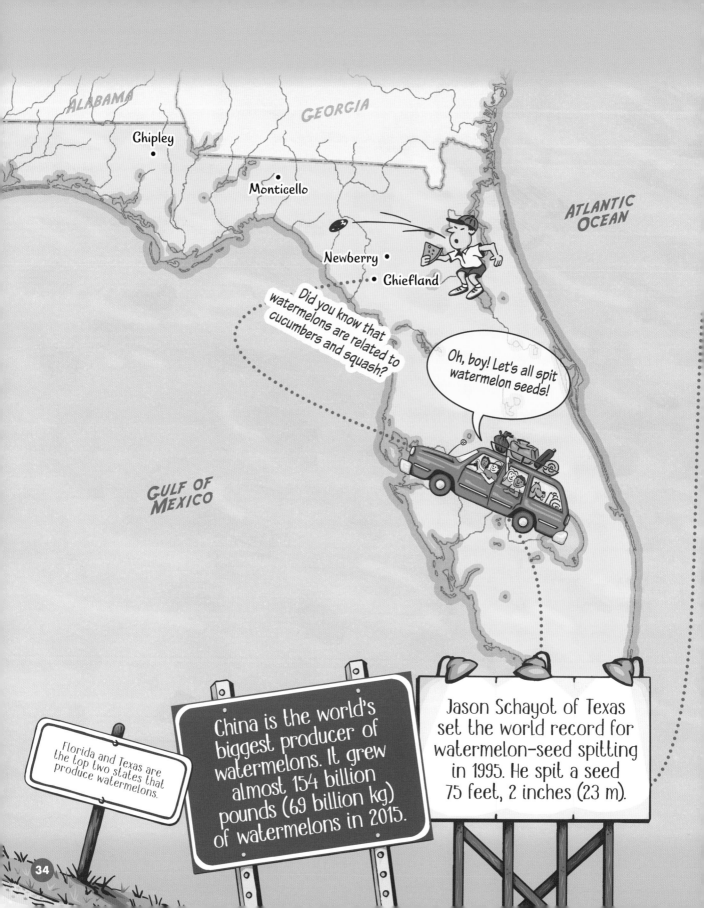

THE WATERMELON FESTIVAL IN CHIEFLAND

Thwit! Darn. That one hit a tree. Thwat! Oops. That one hit a dog. Are you any better at spitting watermelon seeds? Then come to the Chiefland Watermelon Festival!

Watermelons are an important Florida crop. Several Florida towns have watermelon festivals. They include Chiefland, Monticello, Chipley, and Newberry. Their seed-spitting contests are big hits. So are the melon-eating contests.

So how far can you spit a seed? Warning: Don't try it at home!

Hungry? Dig into a watermelon in Chiefland!

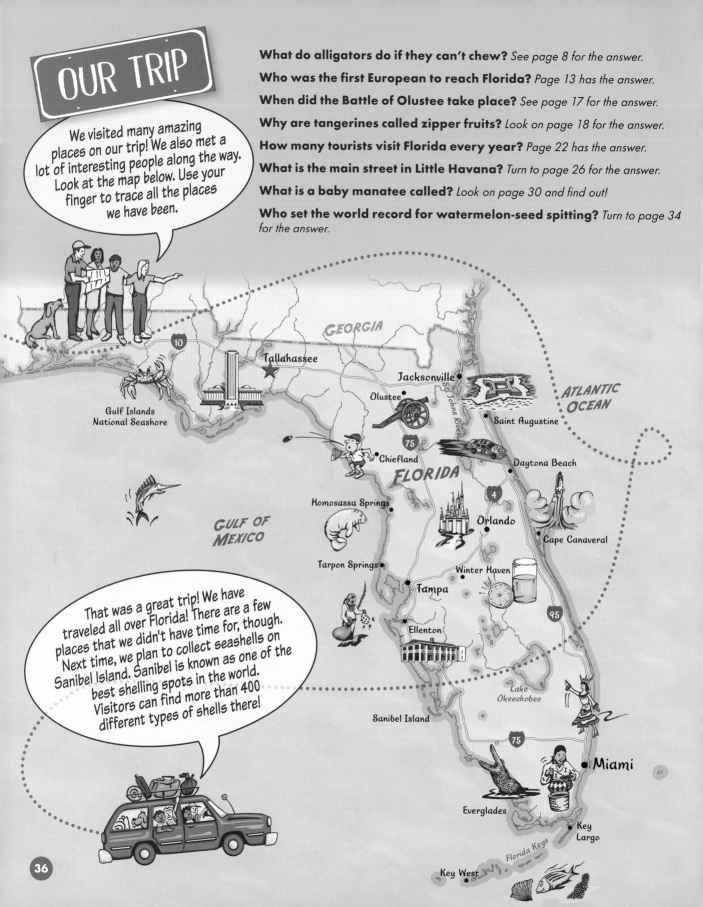

OUR TRIP

We visited many amazing places on our trip! We also met a lot of interesting people along the way. Look at the map below. Use your finger to trace all the places we have been.

What do alligators do if they can't chew? *See page 8 for the answer.*

Who was the first European to reach Florida? *Page 13 has the answer.*

When did the Battle of Olustee take place? *See page 17 for the answer.*

Why are tangerines called zipper fruits? *Look on page 18 for the answer.*

How many tourists visit Florida every year? *Page 22 has the answer.*

What is the main street in Little Havana? *Turn to page 26 for the answer.*

What is a baby manatee called? *Look on page 30 and find out!*

Who set the world record for watermelon-seed spitting? *Turn to page 34 for the answer.*

That was a great trip! We have traveled all over Florida! There are a few places that we didn't have time for, though. Next time, we plan to collect seashells on Sanibel Island. Sanibel is known as one of the best shelling spots in the world. Visitors can find more than 400 different types of shells there!

GEORGIA

Tallahassee

Jacksonville

Olustee

St. Johns River

Saint Augustine

ATLANTIC OCEAN

Gulf Islands National Seashore

Chiefland

FLORIDA

Daytona Beach

GULF OF MEXICO

Homosassa Springs

Orlando

Cape Canaveral

Tarpon Springs

Winter Haven

Tampa

Ellenton

Lake Okeechobee

Sanibel Island

Everglades

Miami

Key Largo

Florida Keys

Key West

STATE SYMBOLS

State animal: Florida panther

State beverage: Orange juice

State bird: Mockingbird

State butterfly: Zebra longwing

State flower: Orange blossom

State freshwater fish: Largemouth bass

State gem: Moonstone

State marine mammal: Manatee

State reptile: Alligator

State saltwater fish: Atlantic Sailfish

State saltwater mammal: Dolphin

State shell: Horse conch

State stone: Agatized coral

State tree: Sabal palm

State wildflower: *Coreopsis*

STATE SONG

"THE SWANEE RIVER"
(ALSO CALLED "OLD FOLKS AT HOME")
Words and music by Stephen C. Foster

Way down upon the Swanee
  River,
Far, far away,
There's where my heart is turning
  ever,
There's where the old folks stay.
All up and down the whole
  creation
Sadly I roam,
Still longing for the old plantation,
And for the old folks at home.

Chorus:
All the world is sad and dreary,
Everywhere I roam;
Oh, brothers, how my heart
  grows weary,
Far from the old folks at home!

All 'round the little farm
I wander'd

When I was young,
Then many happy days
I squander'd,
Many the songs I sung.
When I was playing with my
  brother
Happy was I;
Oh, take me to my kind old
  mother!
There let me live and die.

One little hut among the bushes,
One that I love,
Still sadly to my memory rushes,
No matter where I rove.
When will I see the bees a
  humming
All 'round the comb?
When shall I hear the banjo
  strumming,
Down in my good old home?

State seal

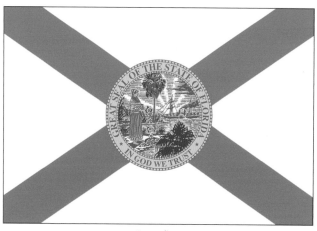

State flag

FAMOUS PEOPLE

Arnaz, Desi (1917–1986), musician and television star

Bethune, Mary McLeod (1875–1955), educator and reformer

Bush, Jeb (1953–), former governor

Carlton, Steve (1944–), former baseball player

Derulo, Jason (1989–), pop and R&B singer

Edison, Thomas Alva (1847–1931), inventor

Estefan, Gloria (1957–), singer

Hemingway, Ernest (1899–1961), author

Homer, Winslow (1836–1910), artist

Hurston, Zora Neale (1891–1960), author

Johnson, James Weldon (1871–1938), author, civil rights leader

McQueen, Butterfly (1911–1995), actor

Moore, Mandy (1984–), actress and singer-songwriter

Morrison, Jim (1943–1971), rock star

Osceola (ca. 1800–1838), Seminole chief

Pérez, Armando "Pitbull" (1981–), rap artist

Poitier, Sidney (1927–), actor

Ponce de Léon, Juan (1460–1521), explorer

Rawlings, Marjorie Kinnan (1896–1953), author

Reno, Janet (1938–), former attorney general

Ringling, John (1866–1936), circus owner

Robinson, David (1965–), former basketball player

Rubio, Marco (1971–), U.S. senator

Stowe, Harriet Beecher (1811–1896), author

Tebow, Tim (1987–), professional baseball player and former professional football player

Versace, Gianni (1946–1997), fashion designer

WORDS TO KNOW

arepas (uh-RAY-pas) grilled cornmeal cakes

diploma (duh-PLOH-muh) a paper that says someone has completed a grade or a school

dome (DOHM) a rounded form on top of a building

fertilizer (FUR-tuh-lize-ur) plant food

habitats (HAB-uh-tats) the places and natural conditions in which a plant or an animal lives

Hispanic (hiss-PAN-ik) having roots in Spanish-speaking lands

immigrants (IM-uh-gruhnts) people who leave their home country for a new country

industries (IN-duh-streez) types of business

mansion (MAN-shuhn) a very large, fancy house

marshland (MARSH-land) a region of soft, wet land with grasses growing in it

merengue (muh-RAYN-gay) a dance from Haiti and the Dominican Republic

peninsula (puh-NIN-suh-luh) an area of land that is mostly surrounded by water

reservation (rez-ur-VAY-shuhn) land set aside for use by a group such as Native Americans

skyscraper (SKYE-skray-pur) a very tall, narrow building

swamps (SWAHMPS) wetlands

TO LEARN MORE

IN THE LIBRARY
Conklin, Wendy. *The Seminoles of Florida: Culture, Customs, and Conflict.*
Huntington Beach, CA: Teacher Created Materials, 2016.

Jerome, Kate Boehm. *Florida: What's So Great About This State?* Charleston, SC: Arcadia Publishing, 2010.

Marsh, Laura. *Alligators and Crocodiles.* Washington, DC: National Geographic's Children's Books, 2015.

ON THE WEB
Visit our Web site for links about Florida:
childsworld.com/links

*Note to Parents, Teachers, and Librarians: We routinely verify our Web links to make sure
they are safe and active sites. So encourage your readers to check them out!*

PLACES TO VISIT OR CONTACT
Florida Tourism Centers
visitflorida.com
751829 I-95
Yulee, FL 32097
904/225-9182
For more information about traveling in Florida

HistoryMiami Museum
historymiami.org
101 West Flagler Street
Miami, FL 33130
305/375-1492
For more information about the history of Florida

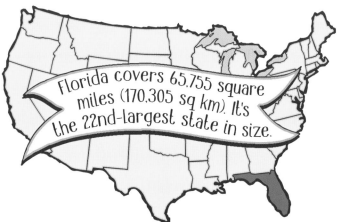

Florida covers 65,755 square miles (170,305 sq km). It's the 22nd-largest state in size.

INDEX

Bye Sunshine State.
We had a great time.
We'll come back soon!